Town Farms

Written by Jan Burchett and Sara Vogler

Collins

You can visit this farm near a town.

3

The ducks dip down for food.

Bees buzz and look for nectar. Nectar is food for bees.

This is a bee expert.

Get seeds at the farm shop and feed the chickens.

8

Feed the goats too.

The goats push at
the food pan.

You can pet the rabbits and feed them carrots.

Up high, you can get a good look at the farm!

It is fun to visit a town farm.

In the farm shop

On the farm

At ten, gather eggs.

Then meet the goats.

Feed the cows and sheep.

The farm

🐾 Review: After reading 🐾

Use your assessment from hearing the children read to choose any GPCs, words or tricky words that need additional practice.

Read 1: Decoding
- Point to the word **expert** on page 7. Discuss its meaning by looking at the whole sentence and the picture. Ask: What is an expert? (e.g. *a person who knows a lot about a subject*) What does this expert know about? (*bees*) What clues show he is a bee expert? (e.g. *his special outfit*)
- Encourage the children to sound out and blend the words, e.g. **r/a/bb/i/t/s**. It may help to point to the sounds as they read these words:

   good   food   nectar   down   seeds   near   goats   carrots

- Point to words with long vowel sounds. Say: Can you blend in your head when you read these words?

Read 2: Prosody
- Model reading pages 14–15 as if you are narrating a television advert.
- Challenge the children to read the pages with enthusiasm. Say: Can your reading voice persuade more visitors to come to the farm?

Read 3: Comprehension
- Turn to pages 12 and 13 and ask the children if they have been to a farm, or petted animals like this. Ask them to describe their animal experiences.
- Read page 2. Point to **you**, and ask who is meant by this word. (*the readers*) Discuss how non-fiction authors are more likely to use "you". Compare with the use of "he"/"she" in fiction books.
- Turn to pages 22 and 23. Ask questions to encourage the children to describe and explain the pictures:
   o Where is the farm? (*a town*) Is there a clue that this is true in one of the pictures? (*buildings, top left*)
   o How do the ducks find food? (*by dipping down under water*)
   o Which animals eat seeds? (*chickens/goats*) How do you know the goats like seeds? (*they* **push at the food pan**)
- Bonus content: Turn to pages 16 and 17. Ask the children to use the pictures to predict what else people can see and help with on the farm. Ask: Where do the items in the farm shop come from? How do you think they are made?
- Bonus content: Turn to pages 18 to 21. Using the voice of an announcer at the farm, read the text and look at the clocks to tell everyone what they can do and when.